I Am Jesus' Little Lamb

God's Promises at Baptism

Laura Langhoff Arndt

ISBN: 1545209065
ISBN-13: 978-1545209066

Dedication

This book, as well as my whole life, is dedicated to God, the Father, the Son, and the Holy Spirit, who has given me the ability and desire to do this and all things.

Acknowledgments

Thanks to my husband, Kevin, who loves Jesus more than he loves me, makes sure I don't publish heresy, and teaches me something new every time we talk about God or His Word.

Baptism (washing with water) is not just water, but water combined with God's word.

When we are baptized, God promises us great things.

God created you and chose you!

Born:

Baptized:

Attach Photo Here

Jesus said, "Let the little children come to me and do not hinder them, for to such belongs the kingdom of heaven."
Matthew 19:14

Godparents or Sponsors

Sponsors are special friends chosen by your parents to help you.

Their important job is to:

1) Be at your baptism and watch it happen.
2) Pray for you.
3) Support and encourage you to go to church and learn about the Bible and Jesus in Sunday School.
4) Be examples of living a life of faith, following Jesus.

Your sponsors are:

When You Were Baptized

The Father, and the Son, and the Holy Spirit

When you were baptized, your parents, and your godparents stood around a large bowl of water. The pastor made the sign of the cross on your forehead and on your heart. Somebody held you over the water and the pastor poured water on your forehead three times, baptizing you in the name of the Father, and of the Son, and of the Holy Spirit.

Go therefore and make disciples of all nations, baptizing them in the name of the Father and of the Son and of the Holy Spirit,
Matthew 28:19

When You Were Baptized

The Father, and the Son, and the Holy Spirit

There were prayers said for you and your godparents, and the pastor may have given you a lit candle to show that you had received Jesus, the Light of the world, or a white cloth to show the holiness of Jesus.

After all this was said and done, you were welcomed into the Family of Christ by the whole congregation and all the angels in heaven were happy!

Again Jesus spoke to them, saying, "I am the light of the world. Whoever follows me will not walk in darkness, but will have the light of life."
John 8:12

God's Promises at Baptism

Receive the Holy Spirit

Jesus was baptized in the river by John. When it was over the clouds opened up and he received the Spirit of God. We call him the Holy Spirit. When we are baptized we receive the Holy Spirit too.

When Jesus was baptized, immediately he went up from the water, and behold, the heavens were opened to him, and he saw the Spirit of God descending like a dove and coming to rest on him; and behold, a voice from heaven said, "This is my beloved Son, with whom I am well pleased."
Matthew 3:16-17

God's Promises at Baptism

Receive the Holy Spirit

We cannot see the Holy Spirit because he surrounds us like the air. We don't see it, but we know it's there because we keep breathing. We know the Holy Spirit is there because God tells us he is. The Spirit teaches us about God, grows our faith, and reminds us of all that Jesus has said and done. He even prays for us when we don't know what to say.

And Peter said to them, "Repent and be baptized every one of you in the name of Jesus Christ for the forgiveness of your sins, and you will receive the gift of the Holy Spirit.
Acts 2:38

God's Promises at Baptism

Forgiveness of Sins

God, who created us, loves us, and takes care of us, is perfect and holy. When we do things God doesn't like, we become dirty. This dirt is called sin and it keeps us away from him. It makes us feel bad, ashamed, embarrassed, afraid of being in trouble, or sad. Baptism washes the sin and bad feelings away and makes us clean. That's called forgiveness.

And now why do you wait? Rise and be baptized and wash away your sins, calling on his name.'
Acts 22:16

God's Promises at Baptism

Eternal Salvation

Because you are baptized, one day Jesus will welcome you into his kingdom in heaven. You will be with your family and friends who believe. The Bible says Jesus has a special room saved just for you. There will be a great party when you get there!

"Fear not, little flock, for it is your Father's good pleasure to give you the kingdom."
Luke 12:32

My New Family

One of His Flock

When you were baptized, God made you one of his own. He adopted you into his family and placed his name on you. He gave you the name, Christian.

For in one Spirit we were all baptized into one body—Jews or Greeks, slaves or free—and all were made to drink of one Spirit.

1 Corinthians 12:13

My New Family

One of His Flock

Shepherds take care of sheep.
Jesus is our shepherd.
We are his sheep.

I am Jesus' little lamb,
Ever glad at heart I am;
For my Shepherd gently guides me,
Knows my need, and well provides me,
Loves me every day the same,
Even calls me by my name.

My New Family

One of His Flock

Jesus knew you before you were born. He knows everything about you. He even knows how many hairs are on your head!

Jesus wants to lead us our whole lives. He gives us peace and joy, strength and courage, and everything we need to live.

Day by day, at home, away,
Jesus is my staff and stay.
When I hunger, Jesus feeds me,
Into pleasant pastures leads me;
When I thirst, He bids me go
Where the quiet waters flow.

My New Family

One of His Flock

Baptism is one of the special gifts God gives us. It is one of the ways God shows that he loves us and it comes with great promises. One thing you can count on is that God keeps his promises, always and forever

.

Who so happy as I am,
Even now the Shepherd's lamb?
And when my short life is ended,
By His angel host attended,
He shall fold me to His breast,
There within His arms to rest.

My New Family

One of His Flock

Once it is given, in the name of the Father, the Son, and the Holy Spirit, baptism is yours forever. You never have to do it again. You have been given the Holy Spirit, your sins are washed away, and if you keep believing these promises you get to go to heaven to be with Jesus when your body gets old and dies.

How do we thank God for this wonderful gift?

Jesus answered, "Truly, truly, I say to you, unless one is born of water and the Spirit, he cannot enter the kingdom of God.
John 3:5

My New Family

One of His Flock

We thank God by going to church to worship him. That's when people get together to read the Bible, pray (when we talk to God), sing songs, and the pastor talks to us about the Bible. When we go home from church we feel happy because we have been reminded of God's promises and how much he loves us.

And Jesus answered him, "It is written, "'You shall worship the Lord your God, and him only shall you serve.'"
Luke 4:8

My New Family

One of His Flock

We also thank God by telling other people about the gift of baptism so they can have the same promises and be sheep like us!.

And he said to them, "Go into all the world and proclaim the gospel to the whole creation. Whoever believes and is baptized will be saved, but whoever does not believe will be condemned.

Mark 16:15-16

My New Family

One of His Flock

Baptism is the first step in your life of faith. When you are old enough you will go to Sunday School. When you learn to read you will be able to read the Bible yourself. Later, you will take a class called Confirmation where you will learn a lot more about Jesus, your shepherd, and being one of his sheep. Grown-ups learn about God and the Bible too. It's fun to learn about God!

Make me to know your ways, O Lord; teach me your paths. Lead me in your truth and teach me, for you are the God of my salvation; for you I wait all the day long.

Psalm 25:4-5

Rejoice!

At baptism, God promises you the Holy Spirit, forgiveness of sins, and heaven, and he always keeps his promises! What could be better than that?

I Am Jesus' Little Lamb

by Henrietta L. von Hayn, 1724-1782

I am Jesus' little lamb,
Ever glad at heart I am;
For my Shepherd gently guides me,
Knows my need, and well provides me,
Loves me every day the same,
Even calls me by my name.

Day by day, at home, away,
Jesus is my staff and stay.
When I hunger, Jesus feeds me,
Into pleasant pastures leads me;
When I thirst, He bids me go
Where the quiet waters flow.

Who so happy as I am,
Even now the Shepherd's lamb?
And when my short life is ended,
By His angel host attended,
He shall fold me to His breast,
There within His arms to rest.

For the Parents

This section explains some biblical truths about baptism. It is not intended to provide a comprehensive understanding of baptism or cover all the possible questions that might arise. For further information see Luther's Large and/or Small Catechism.

For the Parents

Baptism is a Gift
Some people consider baptism an outward sign of an inward change, or a pledge or commitment we make to acknowledge our faith. They think it is something we do for God; a symbol of a choice we have made to be saved instead of something God does for us. But, baptism is actually something God does for us. It is a gift freely given out of love, not earned. It is given with no expectations upon the recipient. It's one of the ways God gives us his grace.

He saved us, not because of works done by us in righteousness, but according to his own mercy, by the washing of regeneration and renewal of the Holy Spirit, whom he poured out on us richly through Jesus Christ our Savior. (Titus 3:5-6)

Gifts of Baptism
Baptism is not just a ritual or tradition. Through it, God gives us 1) the gift of the Holy Spirit, 2) forgiveness of sins, 3) he rescues us from death and the devil, and 4) gives us eternal salvation. With those gifts, parents have the assurance of salvation for all of their kids, even a baby.

He has delivered us from the domain of darkness and transferred us to the kingdom of his beloved Son, in whom we have redemption, the forgiveness of sins. (Colossians 1: 13-14)

And Peter said to them, "Repent and be baptized every one of you in the name of Jesus Christ for the forgiveness of your sins, and you will receive the gift of the Holy Spirit.
For the promise is for you and for your children and for all who are far off, everyone whom the Lord our God calls to himself." (Acts 2:38-39)

For the Parents

A Gift of Grace
Baptism is one of the ways God offers us his grace; forgiveness of sins and salvation. It's important to realize that there is nothing we can do to earn our way to heaven. Grace comes to us through the hearing of the Word of the gospel, baptism, and the Lord's Supper. It is by God's grace and the death and resurrection of Jesus Christ that we are forgiven and have eternal life.

For by grace you have been saved through faith. And this is not your own doing; it is the gift of God, not a result of works, so that no one may boast. (Ephesians 2:8-9)

But if it is by grace, it is no longer on the basis of works; otherwise grace would no longer be grace. (Romans 11:6)

One Baptism
Baptism, if done with water and Christ's words (in the name of the Father, and of the Son, and of the Holy Spirit), should not be repeated. Nobody should be re-baptized because they think they need to do so to recommit themselves to following Christ. The only time somebody should be re-baptized is if they were baptized in a church that doesn't recognize the three persons of God (Trinity - Father, Son, Spirit) or if they are not sure they were baptized in that way.

Christ loved the church and gave himself up for her, that he might sanctify her, having cleansed her by the washing of water with the word. (Ephesians 5:25-26)

One Lord, one faith, one baptism. (Ephesians 4:5)

For the Parents

Baptizing Babies

When Adam and Eve sinned, they separated themselves, and everyone after them, from God. Therefore, anyone born after them was born in a sinful state, separated from God. Some people think babies cannot sin until they understand sin, but sin involves more than just what we do. Being born in a sinful state/separation, babies need the gifts of baptism.

Behold, I was brought forth in iniquity, and in sin did my mother conceive me.
(Psalm 51:5)

Also, the Bible says to baptize "every one of you," and "all nations," and "whole households." It does not say to baptize all nations except for the babies. Jesus does, however, tell the disciples to let the children come to him. (Acts 2:38-39, Matthew 28:19, Acts 16:13-15)

Now they were bringing even infants to him that he might touch them. And when the disciples saw it, they rebuked them. But Jesus called them to him, saying, "Let the children come to me, and do not hinder them, for to such belongs the kingdom of God. (Luke 18:15-16)

Some people think babies cannot have faith until they can understand faith. Faith, however, is not an intellectual activity. It is not something that is accepted or earned by us. Babies are given faith when they hear the word.

Yet you are he who took me from the womb; you made me trust you at my mother's breasts. On you was I cast from my birth, and from my mother's womb you have been my God.
(Psalm 22: 9-10)

For the Parents

Sponsors

Baptism is not a ritual, symbol, or ceremony to determine guardianship of children should anything happen to their parents or a life coach, as is commonly thought today. When parents choose to have their child baptized, they are saying that they acknowledge that their child was born in sin and that they want him/her to have the gifts from God that baptism brings. Sponsors should be sincere Christians who consider themselves privileged to be chosen for this sacred and solemn obligation. When choosing a sponsor, parents should keep in mind the role a godparent plays in the spiritual life and welfare of the child.

Confess the Faith

Sponsors are expected to share and confess the faith conveyed in the Apostles' Creed and taught in Luther's Small Catechism.

Witness

Sponsors serve as witnesses that those who receive the Sacrament of Baptism have been properly baptized in the name of the Father, the Son, and the Holy Spirit.

Prayer

Sponsors are to pray regularly for the faith and protection of their godchildren.

Christian Education

Sponsors, in the case of children, support and encourage them in their ongoing Christian education and participate in nurturing their faith. Should the parents fail or die, the sponsor should make every effort to carry out this important part of faith development.

For the Parents

Worship
Sponsors are to encourage their godchildren in instruction of the Lord's Supper, and continued worship.

Living Examples
Sponsors are to be examples of a life lived in faith. Should their godchild stray from their faith and church, they should advise repentance.

Luther's Small Catechism states:
"Only those of the same confession of faith should be sponsors."

Having godparents who have different beliefs from their godchildren puts them in a difficult position. At baptism they are asked to take vows to support raising the child in the faith of the parents. If they have different religious views and convictions, they may not be able to carry out this charge in good conscience.

Parent's Duty at Baptism
Parents should not forget their own spiritual or faith journey while they encourage their children. They should develop personal habits that include Bible study and prayer, worship as a family, and attendance in Bible study while their children attend Sunday School. Be sure to read the Bible and pray together at home. Live a life of faith and your child will too.

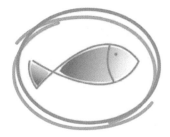

About the Author

Laura Langhoff Arndt taught secondary education for over 15 years, has an M.A. in Classroom Instruction, and is certified as a Director of Christian Education in the Lutheran Church – Missouri Synod. She also enjoys painting watercolors and riding her bike.

She is the author of *The Art of Teaching Confirmation*, a book about how to most effectively teach confirmation to middle school students, and creates free educational resources on her blog, The Carpenter's Ministry Toolbox.

Then I heard the voice of the Lord saying, "Whom shall I send? And who will go for us?" And I said, "Here am I. Send me!" Isaiah 6:8

Made in the USA
Coppell, TX
02 July 2022

79488480R00021